Endpaper: A page from an Aztec calendar almanac.

SEE INSIDE

AN AZTEC TOWN

Author: Cottie Burland.

SERIES EDITOR
R.J. UNSTEAD

WARWICK PRESS

Series Editor
R. J. Unstead
Author
Cottie Burland, FRAI
Editor
Adrian Sington
Illustrations
Charlotte Snook
Maurice Wilson
Ron Jobson
Rob McCaig
Temple Art

Published by Warwick Press, 730 Fifth Avenue,
New York, New York, 10019.

First published in Great Britain by Hutchinson
and Co Ltd in 1980.

Copyright © 1980 by Grisewood & Dempsey Ltd.

Printed by South China Printing Co
Hong Kong.

6 5 4 3 2 1   All rights reserved

Library of Congress Catalog No. 80-50041

ISBN 0-531-09173-2

CONTENTS

City of the Swamps	8
The Temple of Death	10
The Royal Palace	12
The Law of the Gods	14
Strict Upbringing	15
The Craftsmen Elite	16
Tlatelolco Market	18
Farming the Swamps	20
Law, Order and the Empire	22
A Warrior's Life	24
End of the Civilization	26
Important Happenings	27
Glossary	28
Index	29

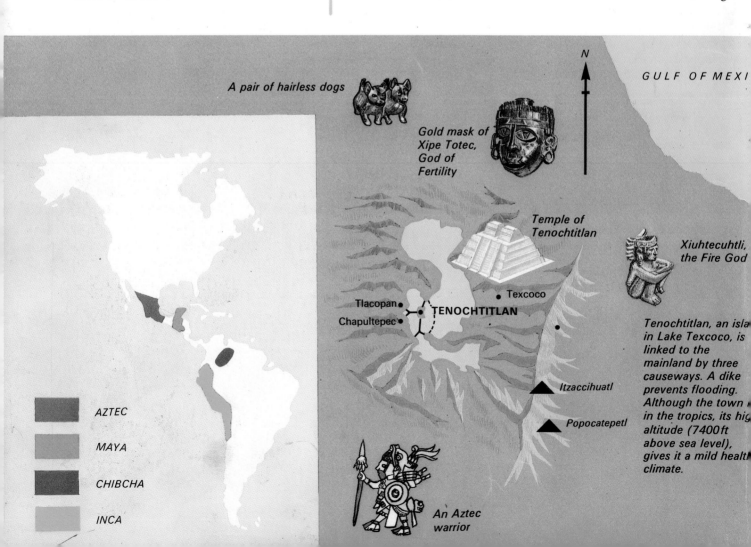

A pair of hairless dogs

Gold mask of Xipe Totec, God of Fertility

N

GULF OF MEXI

Temple of Tenochtitlan

Xiuhtecuhtli, the Fire God

Tlacopan

Texcoco

TENOCHTITLAN

Chapultepec

Itzaccihuatl

Popocatepetl

Tenochtitlan, an isla
in Lake Texcoco, is
linked to the
mainland by three
causeways. A dike
prevents flooding.
Although the town
in the tropics, its hig
altitude (7400 ft
above sea level),
gives it a mild health
climate.

AZTEC

MAYA

CHIBCHA

INCA

An Aztec warrior

The Rise of the Aztecs

By 1500, the Aztec empire stretched across Mexico from the Atlantic to the Pacific coast. With its capital in Tenochtitlan, a town of half a million people, it was the most powerful civilization in Central America.

Mexico is a land of mountains and valleys; the greatest of which is the Valley of Mexico. Here, at about the time of the birth of Christ, the ancestors of the Aztecs made their first appearance. The Olmecs and Zapotecs lived in the shadow of several volcanoes. Their descendants migrated north and from AD 300 to 600 the Valley was dominated by the great city of Teotihuacan.

The people who appear most in Aztec legends are the Toltecs. Tollan, their capital, was thought to be a paradise where crops were plentiful and amaranth plants grew as tall as trees. But the Toltecs were a cruel race who held sway over Mexico until the 12th century. Their carvings are of demon gods. Human sacrifice became a nightly ritual. In 1200 Tollan was sacked and all trace of the Toltecs was destroyed.

Barbarians now roamed into the Valley. In 1168, the Aztec tribe arrived. They were enslaved by the king of Azcapotzalco and made to fight for him. The Aztecs were savage. On one occasion, they ambushed an enemy, killed them and cut an ear from each corpse. They poured the ears over the king. He was so terrified that he banished them to some rocky islets in the lake. They found a rock on which grew a cactus. On it perched an eagle which the Aztecs took to be an omen that their god had fulfilled his ancient promise to give them power. They built a little temple of reeds and called the place Tenochtitlan – 'Beside Cactus Rock'.

Above: Mexico City today. This modern capital stands on the same site as the Aztec capital, Tenochtitlan. The splendid cathedral is built now where an Aztec Temple once stood.

Below: The ruins of a temple at Cancun. To the right are the remains of the priests' house. The bath house in front of the temple was used by worshipers. Water, thrown against a heated wall, produced steam rather as in a Turkish steam bath.

City of the Swamps

Tenochtitlan was a bustling city of half a million inhabitants, much larger than any European town of the time.

The town started as a few squalid huts built on a rocky outcrop in the middle of a swampy lake. The people who live there are all American Indians. They are short and stocky, the men are rarely more than 1 m 70 cm (5 ft 5 in) tall. They have jet black hair, bronzed skins and wear gaily colored clothes. To give themselves more space, the Aztecs dredged mud from the bottom of the shallow lake and made mud platforms on which they built their homes.

The town is linked by a network of canals. The Aztecs move around the town in flat-bottomed canoes, some of them painted and gilded.

The Aztecs are brilliant engineers. To prevent flooding, a dike 15 km (10 miles) long was built as a gift for Montezuma, the greatest Aztec chief. Causeways linking Tenochtitlan to the mainland are wide enough to allow horsemen to ride three abreast. Aqueducts bring fresh water into the town.

The town is divided into four sectors. In the Teopan quarter can be seen the Royal Palace and the huge Temple Precinct. On the temple, victims are cruelly sacrificed to appease the gods, while music plays and the people dance.

The Aztecs' life revolves around the temple and elaborate rituals performed there.

Fresh water flows from the mainland along an aqueduct. Notice the people in canoes carrying water from the reservoirs to the outskirts of the town.

Tenochtitlan is often shaken by small earthquakes. As most of the town's buildings are small, damage is rare.

This volcano is called Popocatepetl which means 'Smoking Mountain'. It is always snow-capped.

A covered aqueduct bringing freshwater from Coyoacan to the Temple Precinct. The 9-mile long dike prevents salty water from polluting the chinampas—artificial vegetable gardens. They can be seen around the outskirts of the town.

The sacred ball game, tlachtli, is played in a stone court with a rubber ball. The aim is to hit the ball through your opponent's stone ring using only your hips, knees or elbows while lying on the ground. Goals are rare! When a goal is scored, that team wins outright and can claim all the clothes and possessions of the spectators.

Below are the priests' quarters and a school
for young priests. There are also rooms for
fasting and penance. In front of the double
temple, black-painted priests sacrifice their
victims. On the platform are braziers burning
incense and stone statues holding banners of
paper and feathers.

The Temple of Death

The Temple Precinct is 350 m (380 yards) by 300 m (330 yards). Surrounding it is the Serpent Wall, so-called because the outside is carved with images of giant rattlesnakes. At the center stands a 60 m (200 ft) high pyramid. A double staircase leads to two huge wooden temples. On the left is the blue sky temple of Tlaloc, god of rain and good food. On the right stands the temple of the war god, Huitzilopochtli, giver of victory to Aztec armies. There is an altar for sacrifices in front of each temple.

A drum booms somberly during the sacrifice. The victims are prisoners from local tribes captured in battle. There are no guards; to the victims it is an honor to die in this way. Inside the temples are giant idols. The priests climb ladders to pour bowls of human blood and hearts over them. The victims are decapitated and the heads placed on the skull rack to proclaim the power of the Aztecs. The torsos are taken away to feed the palace animals. The hands are a great delicacy reserved for the chiefs. The congregation eat the flesh of the limbs cut into little pieces, so that they can swallow the power of the victims.

The temple with the round tower is very sacred. Once a year a noble family sacrifices one man to Quetzalcoatl, the god of priests. The dead man is thrown into the open mouth, which represents the jaws of hell. This brings the family protection for one year.

As well as houses for the priests and their students, the precinct contains the sacred ball court (see caption). Games play an important part in religious ceremonies. The *volador* ceremony, another religious entertainment, imitates the flight of the gods. Four men dressed as birds are attached by ropes to a platform on top of a pole. The rope is wound around the pole. At a given signal they jump off, the rope unwinds as the men spiral to the ground.

An Aztec knife used for sacrifices. The handle shows the sky god delivering a heart to Huitzilopochtli, the God of the Sun. The Aztecs believe that the sun dies when it sets. For the sun to live again, the "divine liquor" found in human hearts has to be offered to it. Every sunset 100 people are sacrificed. Five priests hold the victim, a sixth plunges the knife into his chest cutting the ribs, breast bone and blood vessels. The heart is removed, held up to the sun and then placed in an "eagle dish" for the gods.

To mask outside smells, the Aztecs have large gardens with flowers. Some roofs are inlaid with sweet-smelling cedar wood. Behind, menageries and aviaries are looked after by hundreds of attendants. There is a separate cage for birds of prey, such as vultures and eagles. They eat 500 turkeys a day!

Canoes full of baskets, papaya (a large orange fruit), bundles of cloth and flowers are being punted to the market. A man is buying a bunch of flowers to make him smell sweetly.

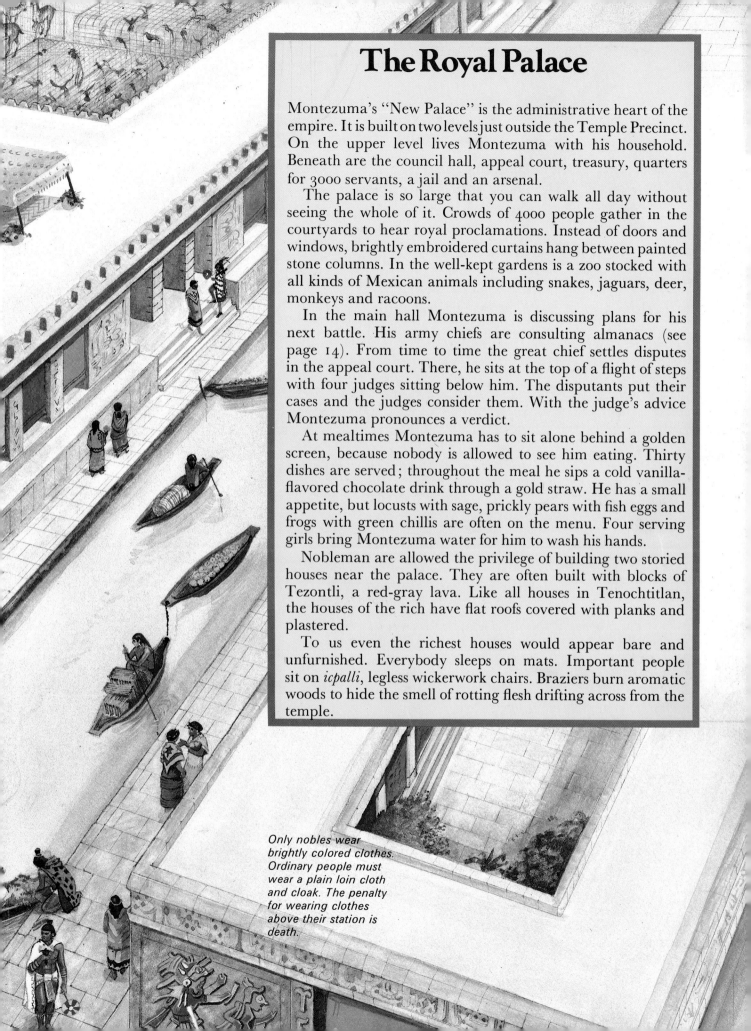

The Royal Palace

Montezuma's "New Palace" is the administrative heart of the empire. It is built on two levels just outside the Temple Precinct. On the upper level lives Montezuma with his household. Beneath are the council hall, appeal court, treasury, quarters for 3000 servants, a jail and an arsenal.

The palace is so large that you can walk all day without seeing the whole of it. Crowds of 4000 people gather in the courtyards to hear royal proclamations. Instead of doors and windows, brightly embroidered curtains hang between painted stone columns. In the well-kept gardens is a zoo stocked with all kinds of Mexican animals including snakes, jaguars, deer, monkeys and racoons.

In the main hall Montezuma is discussing plans for his next battle. His army chiefs are consulting almanacs (see page 14). From time to time the great chief settles disputes in the appeal court. There, he sits at the top of a flight of steps with four judges sitting below him. The disputants put their cases and the judges consider them. With the judge's advice Montezuma pronounces a verdict.

At mealtimes Montezuma has to sit alone behind a golden screen, because nobody is allowed to see him eating. Thirty dishes are served; throughout the meal he sips a cold vanilla-flavored chocolate drink through a gold straw. He has a small appetite, but locusts with sage, prickly pears with fish eggs and frogs with green chillis are often on the menu. Four serving girls bring Montezuma water for him to wash his hands.

Nobleman are allowed the privilege of building two storied houses near the palace. They are often built with blocks of Tezontli, a red-gray lava. Like all houses in Tenochtitlan, the houses of the rich have flat roofs covered with planks and plastered.

To us even the richest houses would appear bare and unfurnished. Everybody sleeps on mats. Important people sit on *icpalli*, legless wickerwork chairs. Braziers burn aromatic woods to hide the smell of rotting flesh drifting across from the temple.

Only nobles wear brightly colored clothes. Ordinary people must wear a plain loin cloth and cloak. The penalty for wearing clothes above their station is death.

The Law of the Gods

The Aztecs worship many gods. The two chief gods are Ometecuhtli and Omecihuatl, the Lord and Lady of creation. Their four sons were responsible for the creation of all the other gods. There are gods for everything: planets, war, hunting, farming, children, flowers and trees. One black godling shakes sleeping dust into children's eyes at sunset. The gods are worshiped at their festivals. At these times they are offered sacrifices of birds and flowers–and of people. In return the gods give success and good health.

The Aztecs have no fear of death. They know that they will return to earth, though in a different form. Where the soul goes after death depends on how a person dies. The most honorable way to die is in battle or by sacrifice. Dead warriors are sent to the Eastern Paradise where they live in flower-filled gardens and fight mock battles. After four years their souls return as hummingbirds or butterflies. Death by drowning is particularly lucky. The dead person is buried and a dry leaf is placed on the grave. When the leaf turns green, the soul has reached the Southern Paradise of Tlaloc, the rain god. Here everything is green and there is plenty to eat. People sing and dance in the gardens. But most people when they die go to the hell of Mictlan, where they dance with other living skeletons, until their turn comes to be reborn again.

Quetzalcoatl, the God of Priests. Priests are educated in the calmecac *schools. Discipline is harsh. Priests are forbidden to marry. As penance, they fast often and cut their ears with cactus spines. A dark green mantle embroidered with skulls hides the priest's black painted body. His hair is never cut, washed or combed, and so it is permanently matted with blood. As messengers of the gods, priests wield tremendous power.*

THE ALMANAC

According to Aztec beliefs everything in life, down to the tiniest detail, is fated. The day and hour of a person's birth determines that individual's fate. There is nothing a person can do to alter fate. It is the will of the gods.

To find out what this fate is, they consult magic books called almanacs. The almanacs show the gods as symbols. Each week, day and hour of the almanac year (there are 20 thirteen-day weeks) is presided over by a different god who acts to form the characters of people born at a particular time. By reading these symbols the Aztecs can see whether a particular day is going to be good or bad.

This almanac shows the week presided over by the god, Xelotl. The little squares on the outside represent the days and hours.

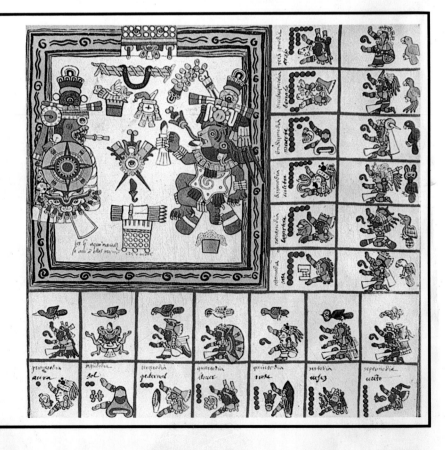

Strict Upbringing

Children of the nobility are very strictly brought up, because in later life they will have to set an example to the masses. They probably envy ordinary children who are not so harshly treated and who spend more time with their parents.

From an early age boys and girls are expected to help around the house. Girls are taught how to use a spindle and how to cook. Boys learn how to handle a canoe, catch fish and make a fire. They look forward to the days spent in the fields keeping birds and animals away from the crops, because there they can run around and play.

If a child is lazy, then he is severely punished. Boys are beaten, pricked by cactus spines and tied up on wet earth for a whole day. In extreme cases their heads are held over a fire of chilli peppers and made to inhale the bitter smoke. Girls have to rise before dawn to do the housework and spend all day sweeping the street outside the house.

Royal children have a very unhappy time. They rarely see their parents except when summoned into the royal chamber. The girls are punished if they raise their eyes from the ground or look behind them. And a boy, even a brother, must never speak to an unmarried woman.

Two kinds of school

Boys and girls go to different schools at the age of seven. There are *calmecac* schools for the noble children and *telpochcalli* schools for the children of peasants and tradesmen. Both are free. *Telpochcalli* pupils are taught subjects that will be useful to them as warriors and citizens. Their food is strictly rationed and they are taught religion, humility and obedience as well as how to use weapons. Music, singing and dancing are taught, because they are important in religious festivals, and not simply for fun.

The *calmecac* schools are like monasteries. They are run by priests (the most educated class in Aztec society). Nobles' sons train here to become high priests. They have to do menial tasks, fast and do penance. At midnight all the boys are roused from their beds to pray and then made to take cold baths. In addition to the subjects taught in the *telpochcalli*, they are taught medicine, mathematics, astronomy, law and writing.

Girls are also taught how to dress and wear makeup. For the Aztecs it is fashionable to have a yellow complexion. Girls rub their cheeks with a yellow cream made from crushed locusts and varnish their feet. Some cut their hair short. Plastering it with black mud and dyeing it with indigo to make it shine is considered very fashionable. Their teeth are dyed with cochineal and their hands and neck are painted with symbols of the gods.

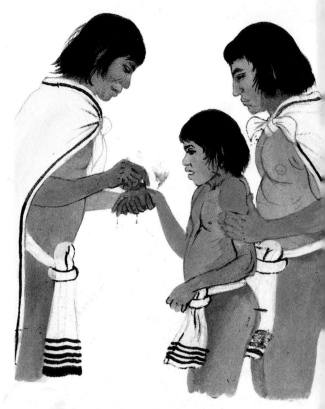

A disobedient boy is punished by being pricked with cactus spines. Afterwards, he will be made to jump into a pool of ice-cold water.

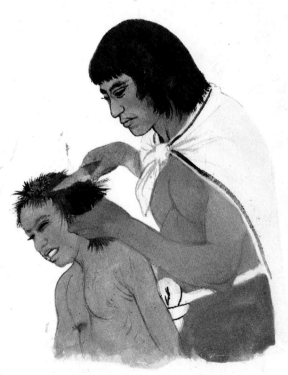

This young warrior is having his head shaved for failing a test at school. The Aztec warriors are punished cruelly, so that they become used to pain.

Crafts

The craftsmen of Tenochtitlan are important people. They live in one section of the town, have their own gods and festivals and rank somewhere between the common people and the ruling classes.

Craftsmen are essential because of the abundance of decoration and ornamentation needed by the Aztecs. All clothes are embroidered or painted. Buildings are sculptured and colored. The temple buildings are filled with feathered images. People paint their faces. There are maps painted on sheets of cloth and almanacs painted in vivid colors. Pottery is painted with mythological designs.

Every design and every color has a symbolic meaning. People love to have different cloaks and face-paint for every occasion. Girls use special pottery stamps to put patterns on their cheeks to show which temple they are going to. Men delight in colorful featherwork ornaments to show their rank. Even the victims for sacrifice are painted and have feathers with tufts of white down in their hair to show that they are going up to the stars.

Making feather headdresses is a difficult process, for no glue is used. Instead, the quills are individually sewn onto a backing and trimmed with gold ornaments.

There is a standard method for painting figures. Every figure has the head in profile, a third of the total height, the body facing forward and the legs in profile. Proportions are carefully measured. No mistakes are allowed or the artist may be sacrificed. The identity of a figure is shown by his dress and color, his position shows what he is doing. Paints are made from crushed minerals and vegetable dyes. Purple is made from a type of snail and red is made from the

Two girls making clothes. One is weaving on a belt-loom, so-called because one end is attached to the weaver by a belt. The other woman is teasing out raw cotton and spinning it into yarn to be used on the loom. The finest cloth is made from cotton imported from plantations in warmer parts of the country. Peasants use leaf fibers and rabbit hair as yarn.

MEDICINE

Illness is thought to be inflicted by the gods as a punishment. Treatment is a mixture of religious chants, sweat baths and herbal drinks administered by an elderly medicine man or woman, the *tititl*. If the case is serious an image of the god Quetzalcoatl is brought in. The image is put beside the invalid and a large quantity of two types of bean are thrown in the air. If they fall mixed together, the patient will recover. If a clear path runs between them, the patient is fated to die. Broken limbs are cleaned by poultices.

crushed bodies of the cochineal insect. About 70,000 of these insects are needed for half a kilogram (1 lb) of dye. Black ink is made from pine soot.

Gold and silver are dredged from river sands, melted and poured into pottery molds to make tools and ornaments such as earrings and collars.

Cotton thread is dyed in different colors then woven to make pictures.

Codices are books which unfold into a single strip. They are made by sticking leather strips together and washing them with lime. Then they are laid out, ready for painting with histories. Usually, the histories have symbols showing who is depicted and the birthday of that person, so that the reader knows the person's fate. This adds to the meaning for those who know the code. Mistakes do occur, usually because they have been painted in a hurry. Some of the histories end in a row of names without any pictures. Perhaps war broke out and the painters had to go off and fight.

Pottery is everywhere. Some is painted, some plain. But all pottery is made without the help of the potter's wheel. The more delicate pots are carefully molded by the hands of an expert who has undergone a long apprenticeship.

Below left: A double-headed serpent made from turquoise and shell, on wood. It is worn by Tlaloc, the Rain God, on his chest. It signifies the coming and going of rain.

Below right: This skull is made from a single block of rock crystal. It is a gift for the gods and represents Mictlantecutli, the Lord of Death.

Making obsidian spearheads. Obsidian—a black volcanic glass—is very brittle. Sudden pressure from a wooden flaking tool on a block of obsidian chips off flakes of razor sharp glass. These are then attached to wooden spear shafts.

Making copper axheads. The craftsman is raising the temperature of the coals by blowing into them. The copper melts and flows into a stone mold.

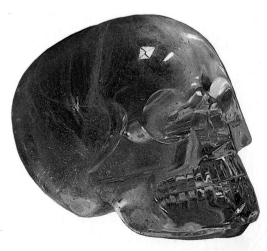

The boats' cargoes of carpets, animals and fruit are being unloaded onto the quayside. In the background, the men with yokes around their necks are being sold as slaves. One is trying to escape. If he reaches the Royal Palace without being caught, he is free. Only the slave's buyer is allowed to chase.

Tlatelolco Market

Tlatelolco is a huge market place, where produce from all over Mexico is sold. People also meet here to exchange gossip and to enjoy themselves. Some people are dancing to the music. Aztec music is full of rhythm. Most of the sound comes from a variety of drums and rattles. Stringed instruments are unknown, only the flute player can play a melody.

The market is under the direct control of Montezuma. So, his representatives often go on a tour of inspection. One of his sons is being carried in a procession. Notice the clothes that the people are wearing. Most wear loin cloths and a cape. The priests, who are waving the censers full of smoking incense, paint their bodies black. Their hair is never cut or washed so it is always caked with blood from the sacrificed victims.

On a dais stands the Lord of the Market. He makes sure that there is fair trading. If a trader is caught selling shoddy goods, he has them confiscated and any false measures are smashed. On the right a court of six sit to try a thief. In the background, a sentenced thief is being beaten to death.

A prince is being carried through Tlatelolco market. All members of the Royal Family are carried in litters by noblemen. No one is allowed to look at Montezuma, on pain of death. Neither can anyone speak to him, except through an official.

Hundreds of items are for sale. Vegetables, fruit, pots and baskets, and fish (meat is a luxury) are always in great demand. Timber, jade, gold, stone for sculpture, skins and feathers are bought by the craftsmen. Quantities of foreign goods are on sale, brought to Tenochtitlan by merchants (see page 22). The merchants travel north to the Pueblo Indians to trade for blue turquoise, southeast to the Maya tribes who grow cocoa beans, south to buy bags of brightly colored parrot feathers, and west to the mountains for gold and silver nuggets.

All items are sold by number or measure, never by weight. There is no money, as such. Everything is bartered, but certain items have agreed values and are used as currency. Mantles, quills full of gold dust and copper ax blades are bartered for expensive items. Cocoa beans are the everyday bartering currency. Thieves sometimes counterfeit cocoa beans out of wax and amaranth dough.

Slaves are also sold in the market. A slave can be bartered for 25 mantles if he is an ordinary slave, or for 35 mantles if he can dance.

Tlatelolco market is close to the Royal Palace and the Temple Precinct. Processions often parade through the Temple around the Palace and finish up in the market place, where everybody sings, dances and praises Montezuma.

Farming the Swamps

Above: Building a chinampa, the Aztecs'
vegetable gardens. The Aztecs are keen
hunters. They spear birds, net fish and wield
an elaborate net to trap birds in flight.

Because Tenochtitlan is in the middle of a lake, the Aztecs rely heavily on their mainland colonies for cotton, crops and food to maintain the temples and armies.

But the poor people of Tenochtitlan have to subsist on the crops they grow on their own plots of land called *chinampas*. *Chinampas* are reed platforms which rest on the lake bottom. Black mud, which is very fertile, from the lake bottom is then poured on top and left to harden. Meanwhile, willow posts are hammered round the *chinampa* edge so that it does not break up.

Before sowing the seed, the plot has to be dug carefully. They use pointed sticks to break up the black soil and make little hillocks for growing corn. Each hillock has five little holes, one for each of the four winds and one in the center for the goddess of growth. A grain of corn is put in each and then

Right: Going to market. The family are
loading their canoe with honey, from the hives
by the house, and rugs. Aztec canoes are
hollowed-out tree trunks. The niche in the
wall is sacred. It houses the image of
Xilonen, the goddess of growth. Every
evening the family ask her to make their
corn plants the highest in the clan. Instead
of a dog, they have a talking parrot to warn
them of intruders.

20

covered over. As the grain grows, the Aztecs pray to the goddess Xilonen. The girls dance for her in their best clothes. When the corn is ripe, they gather the first ears and form a procession. They take the best ears to the temple where they are kept to be resown the following spring.

The farmers also grow vegetables and fruit and always keep a large patch of flowers. The children drive birds and mice from the land. Usually there is a pen near the house for a pair of turkeys. Hairless dogs are kept as pets. At a certain age they are killed and eaten.

Boys make nets which they carry on poles to trap birds, while the men fish the open lake with the nets. They also collect green slime which they make into little edible cakes. A favorite dish is the giant lizard, *iguana*, which tastes like chicken. Frogs are also popular.

Every family has a store house for food in case of famine. Sometimes the famine is so bad that the poorer people have to sell themselves as slaves in exchange for food from the richer landowners. But they can always buy back their freedom with gifts such as piles of blankets and fine pieces of pottery which they make when times are not so hard.

PEASANT HOUSES

Peasants live in wattle and daub huts with a flat straw roof. The room is filled with tools, baskets, spindles for weaving and a stone for grinding the corn. The most sacred part of the room is the hearth. This is a flat clay disk, the *comal*, resting on three stones. On it the wife cooks the corn pancakes, *tortillas* the family's staple food.

The peasant does not own his land, the clan does. Families are given as much land as they need. The land passes from father to son and is returned to the clan only if the family dies out. He also has to pay taxes, in the form of food and cloth, for the upkeep of the state.

Law, Order and the Empire

The law states simply that one has to obey the gods and make regular offerings. There are no jails, only heavy wooden cages in which prisoners are crammed until they are due for sacrifice. Punishments are sudden and often cruel, but people believe that evil acts and their punishment are a matter of fate. They are born to live like that. Stealing is usually punished by giving back three times the amount stolen. If the thief is unable to pay this, then slavery for a time is accepted. But stealing is very rare. People all believe in helping each other for all are members of the same tribe. Slight injuries are compensated for by gifts. But people with serious injuries are often killed because they are no longer able to benefit the tribe.

In the city, people are grouped into *calpulli*, clans living in the same district. The heads of these families meet in council to help one another and to settle disputes. Many serious fights are settled in the *calpulli* courts. A higher court is composed of elected men of different ranks. They meet to discuss more

By moonlight, the merchants return in secret from the Yucatan peninsula. Their canoes, full of jade, tropical feathers and jaguar skins, are hidden from prowlers.

TRIBUTES

All towns in the Aztec empire have to pay tribute in the form of local goods to the government in Tenochtitlan. Every six months the tributes are collected. If the tribute is short, the army takes it by force. The emperor Montezuma records his tributes on codices. Each town has a symbol or glyph down the left side of the page. Quantities and types of goods also have symbols. On the top line is the symbol for Tochtepecan (1), a town 300 km (200 miles) southeast of Tenochtitlan. Next to it is the symbol for blankets (2) and above each blanket is the fir tree symbol which represents 400. So Tochtepecan are giving 2000 blankets, perhaps to keep the Aztec army warm. Below this are symbols for shields (3), tropical birds (4), warrior costumes (5), jade beads (6), 80 bunches of feathers (7) and 40 lip plugs (8).

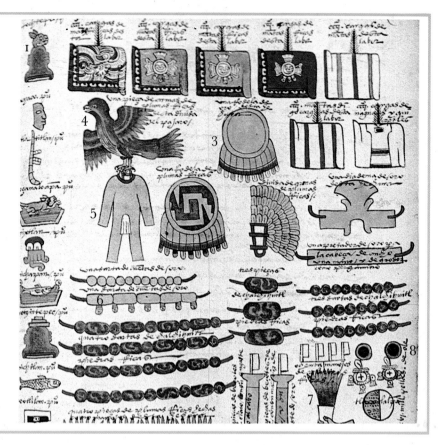

serious disputes. Sometimes they need to adjust land boundaries more fairly. Sometimes they sentence criminals to death. Criminals are killed immediately by drowning or skinning, for it is considered wrong to send criminals as sacrifices to the gods. The most disgraceful crime is for a warrior to run away in battle. He is neither sacrificed nor cremated nor buried. His body is thrown into the swamp, together with the corpses of women of bad reputation. In Mexico the crime of murder is committed because the offender and the victim are fated. It is not the fault of the murderer. It is his fate. Such offenders are taken to the temples and sacrificed to the gods.

The empire is bound together by force. Each colony has to pay a certain amount of tribute (see box). This way, Tenochtitlan, which is so isolated, is able to survive.

Montezuma, helped by his chief official, Snake Woman – a man – is mainly concerned with foreign affairs. He decides the amount of a town's tribute and where to expand the empire.

The tributes are collected by the marauding armies and by traveling merchants, *pochteca*. They travel in large groups and deal only in foreign trade. They form a separate class in Aztec society, have their own courts and live apart, keeping to themselves. On their trading journeys, *pochteca* act as Montezuma's spies, noting the wealth and power of states along the way. Because the Aztecs do not believe in private gain, the *pochteca* have to be careful. If a merchant is met on the road he will deny ownership of his goods. On their return they enter the town at night in secret with covered boats. When in public they dress very plainly.

A Warrior's Life

War is a stage for the Aztecs to show off their power and bully weaker states into submission. It also has a religious purpose. Through war, the Aztec warriors can provide the priests with prisoners for sacrifice to the gods.

From twelve years old, boys are taught to wrestle and fight. At this age they act as porters for the older warriors in battle. From the age of 17 to 22, all Aztec men have to fight for the tribal army. They receive no pay, but the Aztecs consider it the greatest honor to fight for their tribe.

Not until a man has captured three prisoners can he wear his hair in a tuft and call himself a full warrior. Warriors wear sandals, a loin cloth and carry circular shields with leather hangings to catch enemy darts and spears. Some warriors dress in ocelot skins and helmets. They spy on the enemy. Others, such as the warriors dressed as eagles, form the main

Above: A regular soldier hurling a spear with a special thrower.

Above: This warrior is allowed to dress as an Eagle—reward for his bravery.

Left: This fierce warrior is honored to wear his uniform made from jaguar skins.

Right: Training to be a warrior. Boy-porters carry provisions as the army goes out to fight. Young warriors relax in the mountains, by singing and dancing round the camp fire. At the telpochcalli school, boys engage in mock battles using wooden weapons. A young warrior must capture three prisoners in battle and bring them back to Tenochtitlan before he can wear his hair in a tuft—a sign that he is a fully-fledged warrior.

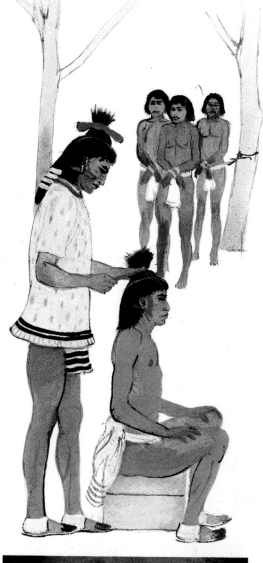

body of fighting men. When the clash comes, the Eagles fight in the center of the unit, while the Ocelots try to outflank the enemy and gash them with wooden clubs edged with obsidian. Prisoners are seized and tied up to be taken away for sacrifice. If the battle is far away prisoners are carried, tied to the backs of their captors.

Some warriors stay with the army after the age of 22, because the rewards can be high. It is possible for a warrior to rise from a common soldier to an army commander if he is brave. Army commanders wear feathered robes, splendid head-dresses and a colored bone through their noses. The supreme commander is Montezuma, sometimes he leads his warriors into battle. He is carried in a palanquin on the shoulders of nobles.

After the battle, a runner is despatched to Tenochtitlan with the result. If the Aztecs have lost he enters the city in silence with his hair loose over his face. If they have won he runs in singing with his hair bound up, to be greeted by flowers, incense and a fanfare of trumpets.

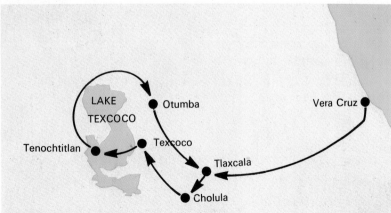

Left: Between April 1519 and August 1521, Cortes and his small army of about 600 conquered Tenochtitlan. From Vera Cruz, he took Tlaxcala and Cholula. He arrived at Tenochtitlan on 15th November 1519, where he was welcomed by Montezuma, who feared that Cortes and his army were white gods. But while Cortes was away, his army attacked the Aztecs. The Aztecs retaliated by driving the Spaniards onto the plain, destroying threequarters of Cortes' army. He retreated. With reinforcements and armed with cannons, he advanced to Tenochtitlan. He cut off the Aztecs' water and food supply. Most of them died and after 80 days, the Aztecs surrendered.

This painting by Diego Rivera (1886–1957) shows Father Miguel Hidalgo y Costilla (right), a Mexican priest, leading the Indians and mestizos (people who are half Spanish and half Indian) against the Spanish (left) in a bid for Independence. Hidalgo was captured and executed by the Spaniards in 1811, but his followers fought on, gaining independence in 1813. The Spaniards returned but eventually granted complete independence to Mexico in 1821.

End of the Civilization

In 1519 Hernan Cortes, a Spanish soldier and adventurer landed on the coast of Mexico and founded the settlement of Vera Cruz. His purpose was to explore the country and to look for treasure. Leaving a few soldiers to guard Vera Cruz, he marched the main body of his *conquistadores* (or conquerors) overland to Tenochtitlan, the splendid capital of the Aztecs. Montezuma, the ruler, received Cortes kindly for he secretly feared the white men and thought Cortes was a god. But Cortes made Montezuma a prisoner and set him up as a puppet governor while the Spanish soldiers plundered the city.

The Aztecs rebelled and chased Cortes' army onto the plains of Otumba. There on 7 July 1520 the Spaniards routed their pursuers. The next year with a reinforced army, the Spaniards recaptured Tenochtitlan, so conquering Mexico. The Aztec nation and its great, though cruel, civilization was at an end.

In 1525 the Aztecs were allowed back into the ruins of their town. The Spaniards had smashed down the old walls and filled in many of the canals. They built a beautiful city of Spanish design. In 1550 they blew up the old pyramid temple with 200 barrels of gunpowder. They cleared the rubble and built a magnificent cathedral on its site.

After the conquest, the Spaniards at first treated the Aztecs well, but as time passed they became little more than slaves. During the period of Spanish rule (which lasted until 1821), the Aztecs were induced to give up the practise of worshiping their old gods and to accept Christianity. Gradually the language and customs of Spain were introduced to the country. Today only about 3000 pure Aztecs remain who speak the old language, Nahuatl.

Mexico today, is a modern democracy with an elected President and government. Its capital, Mexico City, is on the same site as the great Aztec capital, Tenochtitlan.

IMPORTANT HAPPENINGS

200 BC The great pyramids of Teotihuacan are built.

AD
550 Fall of Teotihuacan.
650 Arrival of Toltecs under Quetzalcoatl.
995 The Toltec Civil War.
1000 The Independent city states.
1168 The Aztecs leave Chicomoztoc Valley.

1325 Tenochtitlan founded.
1376 Acamapichtli becomes Chief and captures four towns.
1396-1417 Chimalpopoca fights for independence and conquers two towns.
1427-40 Itzcoatl reigns. Conquers 24 towns.
1440-69 Ueue Montezuma assumes power. He constructs a 15km- (ten-mile) dike. Conquers many tribes.
1496-81 Lordship goes to Axayacatl. He conquers Tlatelolco.
1481-86 Tizoct becomes High Chief. Founds the Great Temple.
1486-1502 Empire reaches the sea.

1502-20 Montezuma, the last High Chief, makes many conquests. Dies 13 July 1520. Cortes conquers Tenochtitlan on 21 November.
1521 The Spanish conquest is complete.
Note: It is said that Itzcoatl altered Mexican history in 1438 in order to suit mythology. So between AD 100 and 1438 dates are uncertain.

The later story of the Spanish conquest has been carefully recorded and it is well worth reading the stories of the long and dreadful struggle in the ruined city of Tenochtitlan.

GLOSSARY OF TERMS

CALMECAC school where boys were trained to be priests.

CHOCOLATL has been adopted by most European languages and means chocolate.

IGUANA a large edible lizard.

MAYA a group of tribes living in Southern Mexico.

MONTEZUMA name of the last Aztec emperor. It means "He of the Strong Arm".

NAHUATL the language spoken by all the valley people except the Otomi. It is a Toltec word meaning speech.

OBSIDIAN volcanic glass used to make blades for weapons.

OCELOT a Mexican wildcat. Warriors dressed up in their skins.

TELPOCHCALLI school where boys trained as warriors.

TLAXCALANS the tribe never conquered by the Aztecs. They helped Cortes conquer the Aztecs.

PICTURE WRITING

1. mountain 2. tree 3. Tenoch-titlan 4. teeth 5. stone 6. Montezuma.

To write, the Aztecs used glyphs—pictures which represent words. If an Aztec wanted to write a word for which it was impossible to draw a picture, such as the name of a town, he would draw two pictures which when spoken together sounded like the town's name. Hence the word Tenoch-titlan is shown by a picture of a cactus (nochtli) and a stone (tetl).

The glyphs were sometimes painted on strips of paper from the bark of a fig tree. They were soaked in lime water, beaten with stone hammers and hung up to dry. The ink was mixed with thick resin so that it did not run on the very soft paper.

AZTEC GODS

CIHUACOATL, goddess of childbirth.

COATLICUE, Earth Goddess and mother of Huitzilopochtli.

HUITZILOPOCHTLI, warrior god, sun god and national god of the Aztecs.

OMETECUHTLI and OMECIHUATL, the first gods, the Lord and Lady of creation.

QUETZALCOATL, god of the wind, god of the creation, god of twins, god of learning.

TEZCATLIPOCA, god of sorcery and darkness.

TLALOC, god of rain. His name means: "He who makes things grow".

TLAZOLEOTL, eater of filth. Penitents confess their sins to him.

TLOQUE NAHUAQUE, Lord of everywhere.

XILONEN, goddess of the young corn plants.

XIPE TOTEC, god of fertility.

YACATECUHTLI, god worshiped by the merchants.

Xochipilli, God of Good Fortune

INDEX

A
almanacs 4, 13, 14, 15, 16
aqueducts 8, 9

C
canals 8, 27
canoes 8, 12, 15, 18, 20, 22, 23
causeways 6, 8
chinampas 9, 20
chocolate 13, 28
clans 16, 20, 21, 22
clothes 8, 13, 16
codices 17, 23
Cortes 26, 27
crops 7, 15, 20, 21
currency 19, 21

D
death 11, 14
dikes 6, 8, 15, 27
discipline 14, 15
dyes 15, 16, 17

F
farming 9, 14, 20, 21
feathers 14, 16, 19, 22, 23, 25
flowers 12, 13, 14, 21, 25
food 9, 13, 19, 21, 26, 28
foreign goods 19, 23

G
games 10, 11
gods 7, 8, 11, 14, 20, 21, 23, 24,
    26, 27, 28

H
hair 8, 14, 15, 16, 18, 24, 25
Hidalgo y Costilla, Father 27
houses 8, 12, 13, 20, 21

Huitzilopochtli 11, 28
hunting 14, 15, 20, 21

I
ink 17, 28

J
justice 13, 18, 22, 23

L
language 27, 28

M
markets 12, 18, 19, 20
Maya 6, 19, 28
medicine 15, 16
merchants 19, 22, 23
Mexico City 7
Montezuma 8, 13, 18, 19, 23, 25,
    26, 27, 28
music 8, 15, 18, 19
musical instruments 11, 18, 19

N
numbers 23

O
obsidian 17, 25, 28
Olmecs 7

P
painting 11, 16, 17, 28
palace 8, 12, 13, 19
paper 11, 28
Popocatepetl 6, 9
pottery 16, 17, 21
priests 7, 11, 14, 15, 18, 24
    clothes 14, 18
punishment 18, 22, 23

Q
Quetzalcoatl 11, 14, 16, 27, 28

S
sacrifices 7, 8, 11, 14, 22, 24, 25,
schools 14, 15, 24, 28
sculpture 7, 11, 16, 19, 20
slaves 18, 19, 21, 22, 27
Snake Woman 23

T
taxes 21
temples 6, 7, 8, 9, 11, 13, 16, 20,
    21, 23
Tlaloc 11, 14, 17, 28
Tlatelolco 18, 27
Toltecs 7, 27
tools 17, 20
tributes 23

V
volador ceremony 11
volcanoes 6, 7, 9

W
war 11, 13, 14, 17, 23, 24, 25, 27
warriors 6, 7, 15, 23, 24, 25
    training 24, 25
    uniforms 23, 24
weaving 15, 16, 21
writing 15, 17, 28
    glyphs 23, 28

X
Xilonen 20, 21, 28
Xipe Totec 6, 28

Z
Zapotecs 7

ACKNOWLEDGEMENTS
Photographs: Endpapers Cottie
Burland; page 7 Alan Hutchinson;
page 11 British Museum; page 14
Cottie Burland; page 17 Cottie
Burland; page 23 Bodleian Library;
page 26 Tony Morrison; page 28
Cottie Burland.